Learn Arabic Alphabets

I Spy with My Little Eye

Plus Tawheed Values and Quran Facts

ANISAH ANISAH

ISBN-13: 978-1-7953-2842-5

Find some magnifying glasses in the pictures and match to the Quran facts on the last page.

This tiny town has all the things we need! Alhamdulillah, Allah gives people the knowledge so they can build all these great architectures. Let's find five letters ج here!

Wow, a lot of letters here!
Can you spot three letters ح
and three letters خ?

Let's explore the underwater world with a submarine! Allah created the ocean and all underwater creatures. We can eat yummy seafood. What letter can we find here? Oh, five letters ر ! Can you spot them?

Next, we have to explore more! Allah created the wonderful underwater scenery so we can enjoy diving and sightseeing. We spy with our little eyes, six letters ز

Now, are you ready to ride the crop duster above the farm? Alhamdulillah, Allah provides us milk, eggs, wools, crops, and many more from the farm. Well, can you find six letters س here?

Do you want to see our animal friends and play hide and seek with them? We are so thankful to Allah for all those beneficial animals. Look, there are some letters hidden. Can you spy six letters ش ?

MaashaAllaah.. so many breads and drinks here. Do you know how amazing Allah created our body and senses? We have a nose to smell food, teeth to munch, a tongue to taste, and a stomach to digest. Anyway, can you spot five letters ص here?

Look at the food! Maashaallaah. They look delicious. Alhamdulillaah. Allah provides us food and drink every single day. Can you find six letters ض ?

ط
ط
ط
ط
ط

All aboard! Choo-choo! Where do you want to go with the train? What kind of train do you like best? Don't forget to make dua before travelling, so Allah will protect us during the journey. Try to spot five letters ط and six letters ظ

Are you sleepy or just want to play your favourite toy? Come to the bedroom and thank Allah for giving us a very comfy and relaxing bedroom. Let's play and find six letters ع here!

Allah created the sun. Sunshine that peeks through the window in the morning makes us really grateful. Alhamdulillaah for the new day. Can you spot six letters غ ?

Mashaallaah.. Have you ever been to a zoo? A lot of animals there! So fun and exciting. Can you spot six letters ف ?

Allah created animals and provides food for them. Which animal is your favorite? A muslim has to love animals. Now, help the kids to find six letters ق here.

Allah created the night and the day, the sun and the moon. Can you spot five letters ك in the dark?

Mashaallah. Think how quiet and peaceful the night is so we may take a rest and how cheerful the day is so we can do many things. Let's explore and find seven letters ل here!

Mashaallaah. Do you know the names of all the planets in our solar system? They are part of a galaxy and there are lots of galaxies in the universe.

Can you help our astronaut friends to find six letters م ?

What a very big universe. People can't explore it all. But, we know for sure, Allah, who created the universe, is The Greatest.

Can you find five letters ن here?

Alhamdulillah, we can enjoy the snow in winter and the beautiful flowers in spring, Now, can you spot six letters و in this picture?

Alhamdulillah, we can enjoy the warmth of summer and the beautiful leaves in autumn. Allah created the sun. Allah created the wind. Allah knows every fallen leaf.
Try to find five letters here!

What a beautiful sky. Maashaallaah. Our friends are exploring the playground. Can you spot six letters ع here?

Wow, so many things to play in the playground with our friends. Which one is your favourite? We have to be thankful to Allah who gives us family, relatives, and friends to talk to and to play with. Help our friends to find six letters ي here!

Qur'an Facts

A. Sura Al-Baqarah 22:
[He] who made for you the earth a bed [spread out] and the sky a ceiling and sent down from the sky, rain and brought forth thereby fruits as provision for you. So do not attribute to Allah equals while you know [that there is nothing similar to Him].

B. Sura Al-Furqan 47:
And it is He who has made the night for you as clothing and sleep [a means for] rest and has made the day a resurrection.

C. Sura Az-Zukhruf 13:
That you may settle yourselves upon their backs and then remember the favor of your Lord when you have settled upon them and say. "Exalted is He who has subjected this to us, and we could not have [otherwise] subdued it.

D. Sura An-Nahl 14:
And it is He who subjected the sea for you to eat from it tender meat and to extract from it ornaments which you wear. And you see the ships plowing through it, and [He subjected it] that you may seek of His bounty; and perhaps you will be grateful.

E. Sura Al-Mu'minun 21:
And indeed, for you in livestock is a lesson. We give you drink from that which is in their bellies, and for you in them are numerous benefits, and from them you eat.

F. Sura Ash-Shu'ara 79:
And it is He who feeds me and gives me drink.

G. Sura An-Naba' 9:
And made your sleep [a means for] rest.

H. Sura al-An'am 97:
And it is He who placed for you the stars that you may be guided by them through the darknesses of the land and sea. We have detailed the signs for a people who know.

I. Sura Al-Jathiya 5:
And [in] the alternation of night and day and [in] what Allah sends down from the sky of provision and gives life thereby to the earth after its lifelessness and [in His] directing of the winds are signs for a people who reason.

J. Sura Al-A'raf 54:
Indeed, your Lord is Allah, who created the heavens and earth in six days and then established Himself above the Throne. He covers the night with the day, [another night] chasing it rapidly; and [He created] the sun, the moon, and the stars, subjected by His command. Unquestionably, His is the creation and the command; blessed is Allah, Lord of the worlds.

K. Sura Al-Hijr 16:
And We have placed within the heaven great stars and have beautified it for the observers.

L. Sura Al-An'am 59:
And with Him are the keys of the unseen; none knows them except Him. And He knows what is on the land and in the sea. Not a leaf falls but that He knows it. And no grain is there within the darknesses of the earth and no moist or dry [thing] but that it is [written] in a clear record.

48928826R00018

Made in the USA
Middletown, DE
16 June 2019